Don't stop UNTIL you're PROUD

Love you

A Queen is not afraid to Fail

Weekly Planner

MEALS / FOOD

MISCELLANEOUS

- REUNIONS/FRIENDS
- IMPORTANT STUFF
- NOTES/REMINDERS
- APPOINTMENTS
- EXERCISE ROUTINE
- FUN STUFF, SHOPPING, ETC

	M	T	W	T	F	S	S

MONDAY

TUESDAY

WEDNESDAY

THURSDAY

FRIDAY

SATURDAY-SUNDAY

I will speak with confidence and self assurance.
I Am Successful, Wealthy & In Good Health.

Every day brings new opportunities.

sunday

monday

tuesday

wednesday

thursday

friday

saturday

to do lists

I have faith in myself.
I am strong and healthy.

Whatever I do, I give my best.

MEALS/FOOD	REUNIONS/FRIENDS	IMPORTANT STUFF	NOTES/REMINDERS	APPOINTMENTS	EXERCISE ROUTINE	FUN STUFF, SHOPPING, ETC

MONDAY

TUESDAY

WEDNESDAY

THURSDAY

					M
					T
					W
					T
					F
					S
					S

MISCELLANEOUS

FRIDAY

SATURDAY-SUNDAY

I am loved and I am wanted.

I have a beautiful imagination.
I LOVE myself.

sunday

monday

tuesday

wednesday

thursday

friday

saturday

to do lists

I have good friends and a wonderful family.

I get better and better every day.
I AM Lucky.

MEALS / FOOD

MISCELLANEOUS

- REUNIONS/FRIENDS
- IMPORTANT STUFF
- NOTES/REMINDERS
- APPOINTMENTS
- EXERCISE ROUTINE
- FUN STUFF, SHOPPING, ETC

M
T
W
T
F
S
S

MONDAY

TUESDAY

WEDNESDAY

THURSDAY

FRIDAY

SATURDAY-SUNDAY

I am grateful for the things I have.

I will achieve all of my goals.

MEALS / FOOD

MISCELLANEOUS

- REUNIONS/FRIENDS
- IMPORTANT STUFF
- NOTES/REMINDERS
- APPOINTMENTS
- EXERCISE ROUTINE
- FUN STUFF, SHOPPING, ETC

M T W T F S S

MONDAY

TUESDAY

WEDNESDAY

THURSDAY

FRIDAY

SATURDAY-SUNDAY

I will accept nothing but the best.

I am constantly improving.

sunday

monday

tuesday

wednesday

thursday

friday

saturday

to do lists

I desire to learn new things.

The little things in life make all the difference.

MEALS / FOOD

MISCELLANEOUS

- REUNIONS/FRIENDS
- IMPORTANT STUFF
- NOTES/REMINDERS
- APPOINTMENTS
- EXERCISE ROUTINE
- FUN STUFF, SHOPPING, ETC

					M
					T
					W
					T
					F
					S
					S

MONDAY

TUESDAY

WEDNESDAY

THURSDAY

FRIDAY

SATURDAY-SUNDAY

My thoughts are positive and full of joy.

I am unique and a gift to the world.

MEALS / FOOD

MISCELLANEOUS

- REUNIONS/FRIENDS
- IMPORTANT STUFF
- NOTES/REMINDERS
- APPOINTMENTS
- EXERCISE ROUTINE
- FUN STUFF, SHOPPING, ETC.

M
T
W
T
F
S
S

MONDAY

TUESDAY

WEDNESDAY

THURSDAY

FRIDAY

SATURDAY-SUNDAY

I am calm and confident.

I am open to new and exciting possibilities.

sunday

monday

tuesday

wednesday

thursday

friday

saturday

to do lists

I am strong, inside and out.

Miracles happen to me.

MEALS / FOOD	REUNIONS/FRIENDS	IMPORTANT STUFF	NOTES/REMINDERS	APPOINTMENTS	EXERCISE ROUTINE	FUN STUFF, SHOPPING, ETC

MONDAY

TUESDAY

WEDNESDAY

THURSDAY

						M
						T
						W
						T
						F
						S
						S

MISCELLANEOUS

FRIDAY

SATURDAY-SUNDAY

I am patient.

I am perfect just the way I am.

MEALS / FOOD

MISCELLANEOUS

REUNIONS/FRIENDS
IMPORTANT STUFF
NOTES/REMINDERS
APPOINTMENTS
EXERCISE ROUTINE
FUN STUFF, SHOPPING, ETC

M
T
W
T
F
S
S

MONDAY

TUESDAY

WEDNESDAY

THURSDAY

FRIDAY

SATURDAY-SUNDAY

I keep my body healthy.

I am important.

sunday

monday

tuesday

wednesday

thursday

friday

saturday

to do lists

I can do anything.

I approve of myself.

MEALS / FOOD

MISCELLANEOUS

- REUNIONS/FRIENDS
- IMPORTANT STUFF
- NOTES/REMINDERS
- APPOINTMENTS
- EXERCISE ROUTINE
- FUN STUFF, SHOPPING, ETC

M T W T F S S

MONDAY

TUESDAY

WEDNESDAY

THURSDAY

FRIDAY

SATURDAY-SUNDAY

I trust my intuition.

My heart guides me.

MEALS / FOOD

MISCELLANEOUS

- REUNIONS/FRIENDS
- IMPORTANT STUFF
- NOTES/REMINDERS
- APPOINTMENTS
- EXERCISE ROUTINE
- FUN STUFF, SHOPPING, ETC

M T W T F S S

MONDAY

TUESDAY

WEDNESDAY

THURSDAY

FRIDAY

SATURDAY-SUNDAY

I am thankful for being who I am.

FAITH. FAMILY. FORGIVENESS.

sunday

monday

tuesday

wednesday

thursday

friday

saturday

to do lists

I support others with love and kindness.

I am a winner.

MEALS / FOOD

MISCELLANEOUS

- REUNIONS/FRIENDS
- IMPORTANT STUFF
- NOTES/REMINDERS
- APPOINTMENTS
- EXERCISE ROUTINE
- FUN STUFF, SHOPPING, ETC

					M
					T
					W
					T
					F
					S
					S

MONDAY

TUESDAY

WEDNESDAY

THURSDAY

FRIDAY

SATURDAY-SUNDAY

GLOW. GRATITUDE. GROW.

I am beautiful.

MEALS / FOOD

MISCELLANEOUS

- REUNIONS/FRIENDS
- IMPORTANT STUFF
- NOTES/REMINDERS
- APPOINTMENTS
- EXERCISE ROUTINE
- FUN STUFF, SHOPPING, ETC

					M
					T
					W
					T
					F
					S
					S

MONDAY

TUESDAY

WEDNESDAY

THURSDAY

FRIDAY

SATURDAY-SUNDAY

I am excited of the unknown.

HOPE. HARMONY. HUMBLE.

MEALS / FOOD

MISCELLANEOUS

- REUNIONS/FRIENDS
- IMPORTANT STUFF
- NOTES/REMINDERS
- APPOINTMENTS
- EXERCISE ROUTINE
- FUN STUFF, SHOPPING, ETC

M
T
W
T
F
S
S

MONDAY

TUESDAY

WEDNESDAY

THURSDAY

FRIDAY

SATURDAY-SUNDAY

I receive all the help that I need.

Everything works out just fine.

MEALS / FOOD	REUNIONS/FRIENDS	IMPORTANT STUFF	NOTES/REMINDERS	APPOINTMENTS	EXERCISE ROUTINE	FUN STUFF, SHOPPING, ETC	

MONDAY

TUESDAY

WEDNESDAY

THURSDAY

FRIDAY

SATURDAY-SUNDAY

MISCELLANEOUS

Exercise routine: M T W T F S S

Wonderful and awesome things happen to me.

IMAGINATION. INSPIRE. INTEGRITY.

MEALS / FOOD

MISCELLANEOUS

- REUNIONS/FRIENDS
- IMPORTANT STUFF
- NOTES/REMINDERS
- APPOINTMENTS
- EXERCISE ROUTINE
- FUN STUFF, SHOPPING, ETC

M T W T F S S

MONDAY

TUESDAY

WEDNESDAY

THURSDAY

FRIDAY

SATURDAY-SUNDAY

I forgive myself for making a mistake.

LOVE. LOYAL. LIFE.

	MEALS / FOOD

MISCELLANEOUS

REUNIONS/FRIENDS	IMPORTANT STUFF	NOTES/REMINDERS	APPOINTMENTS	EXERCISE ROUTINE	FUN STUFF, SHOPPING, ETC
					M
					T
					W
					T
					F
					S
					S

MONDAY

TUESDAY

WEDNESDAY

THURSDAY

FRIDAY

SATURDAY-SUNDAY

I believe in myself.

I believe in my dreams.

MEALS / FOOD

MISCELLANEOUS

- REUNIONS/FRIENDS
- IMPORTANT STUFF
- NOTES/REMINDERS
- APPOINTMENTS
- EXERCISE ROUTINE
- FUN STUFF, SHOPPING, ETC

M T W T F S S

MONDAY

TUESDAY

WEDNESDAY

THURSDAY

FRIDAY

SATURDAY-SUNDAY

I have the courage to be myself.

MIRACLE. MINDFUL. MELLOW.

sunday

monday

tuesday

wednesday

thursday

friday

saturday

to do lists

I am okay with who I am.

What makes you smile?

MEALS / FOOD

MISCELLANEOUS

- REUNIONS/FRIENDS
- IMPORTANT STUFF
- NOTES/REMINDERS
- APPOINTMENTS
- EXERCISE ROUTINE
- FUN STUFF, SHOPPING, ETC

M T W T F S S

MONDAY

TUESDAY

WEDNESDAY

THURSDAY

FRIDAY

SATURDAY-SUNDAY

Write about a place you would like to visit someday?

How can you give back to your community?

MEALS / FOOD

MISCELLANEOUS

- REUNIONS/FRIENDS
- IMPORTANT STUFF
- NOTES/REMINDERS
- APPOINTMENTS
- EXERCISE ROUTINE
- FUN STUFF, SHOPPING, ETC

M T W T F S S

MONDAY

TUESDAY

WEDNESDAY

THURSDAY

FRIDAY

SATURDAY-SUNDAY

MEALS / FOOD

MISCELLANEOUS

REUNIONS/FRIENDS	IMPORTANT STUFF	NOTES/REMINDERS	APPOINTMENTS	EXERCISE ROUTINE	FUN STUFF, SHOPPING, ETC
					M
					T
					W
					T
					F
					S
					S

MONDAY

TUESDAY

WEDNESDAY

THURSDAY

FRIDAY

SATURDAY-SUNDAY

Name 5 things you like about yourself and why.

sunday

monday

tuesday

wednesday

thursday

friday

saturday

to do lists

Made in the USA
Middletown, DE
27 July 2022

70116034R00064